Examining the Armed Citizen:

the Historic Struggle Between Man and the State for Control of Small Arms

*Then said he unto them, But now, he that hath
a purse, let him take it, and likewise his scrip:
and he that hath no sword, let him sell his
garment, and buy one.*

Luke 22:36

A special thank you goes to Nancy Markel and Alex Blake for proofreading this work and many that came before it.

It is one thing to know what you want to say. It is another thing altogether to translate it to the written word.

As with all his previous works, the author suggests that you grab a pencil, highlighter or both before beginning. Highlight sections and take notes in the margins.

Brew coffee and light a cigar if you are so inclined.

Examining the Armed Citizen:

the Historic Struggle Between Man and the State for Control of Arms

Paul G. Markel
Copyright 2018
All Rights Reserved

Examining the Armed Citizen

Introduction

In the United States of America, armed citizens participate in a lifestyle and behavior that is outlawed and denied to most every other person living on planet Earth; they own and carry guns. Even Israel and Switzerland, historically pro-citizen defense, are burdened by the "Condition 3" mentality and have many mandates and license requirements.

Let us examine the term "...to keep and bear arms…" This is a two-fold statement.

Merriam Webster lists the top definition of "keep" as;

a : to retain in one's possession or power

b : to refrain from granting, giving, or allowing

c : to have in control

If we are to accept that our Founding Fathers had a solid grasp on the use of the English language, we can see that, when it comes to arms, we are meant to retain possession, refraining from granting, giving or allowing and to have control.

"Bear arms" means to be in direct control of, or more simply, to carry. The term "torchbearer" is prevalent throughout literature. A torchbearer is not simply a person who owns a torch and keeps it stored in his home for safekeeping. The torchbearer carries the torch, they exercise control over the torch.

Again, Merriam Webster illuminates the use of the word "bear" as a verb;

a : to move while holding up and supporting (something)

b : to be equipped or furnished with (something)

When a state tells a citizens that they are allowed to own a gun, but it must be locked in a safe, separate from ammunition and cannot be transported in a loaded fashion or kept at the ready, "...to keep and bear arms" has been violated. The 2nd Amendment to the United States Constitution does not say "the people can own guns for hunting", it says that the state cannot forbid them from possessing and carrying guns.

Many countries in the world have detailed legislation and mandates that grant the citizen permission to own a firearm. That ownership is accompanied by strict regulations as to the type of gun possessed, where it must be stored, when and where it can be transported, with separate statutes governing the ammunition for the same.

For instance, the people of Australia are still technically allowed to own guns. A friend from "down under" explained that his journey from seeking permission to purchase a gun to actually having it locked up in his personal safe at home took 14 months. The firearm in question was a .22LR target pistol.

Keep in mind, the greater and more broad the state restrictions about the type, design, and configuration of small arms the further from the right to "keep and bear" we go. Additionally, when the state grants its permission to "keep and bear", but puts severe restrictions as to when and where said arms can be borne, and further institutes regulations as to the storage of said arms, what you have is a privilege not an inalienable right.

What we will examine and consider throughout this text is whether or not the ownership of arms is specifically focused on firearms, or all handheld small arms. We will also examine the practical and true definition of an armed citizen.

Also, it should be noted that this discussion will consider "small arms" as man-portable tools that can be wielded and used effectively by an individual. The catapult or trebuchet, mortars and cannons, belt-fed machineguns, etc. are "crew-served weapons" requiring the collective effort of more than one person to employ and use effectively. Yes, we've all seen Rambo run an M60 one-handed, but let's stick to reality. We are not going to lobby for the individual use of the howitzer in these pages. Cannon Rights is a topic for another day.

Lastly, the author understands full well that, as soon as this text becomes public, those who would disagree with the premise of it will register objection. Minions of the all-powerful state will indeed attempt to undermine and relegate the work to the status of mere opinion. Therefore, of all my previous works, this book is the most thoroughly researched and sourced.

Chapter 1   What is an Armed Citizen?

"A free people ought not only to be armed, but disciplined…"

– George Washington, First Annual Address, to both Houses of Congress, January 8, 1790

What is an "armed citizen"? If a person buys a gun does that make them a de facto armed citizen?

To many inhabitants of the world, the concept of being an armed citizen is as foreign or far off to them as walking on the moon. The aforementioned people understand that some men have walked on the surface of the moon, but the idea that they might do the same thing is ridiculous or even absurd. The same thinking applies to owning, and especially carrying, a gun. These folks have seen it in movies and on TV, but the idea that they could carry a firearm, on their person every day, is a concept nearly impossible to imagine.

The previous discussion does not apply only to those living outside of the United States of America, but to those within its borders as well. Many American citizens consider the idea of the armed citizen just as the disarmed tax slaves of the

United Kingdom do; that it is a strange and foreign notion.

Decades of conditioning and psychological normalization have convinced tens of millions of inhabitants of planet Earth that the use and carry of arms by average citizens is not only abnormal, but dangerous. An undeniable divide has been created between those who are "allowed" and "should" have access to arms and those who, for the sake of safety and security, should not be allowed access.

For millions of inhabitants of this world, the mere thought that 'the people' or 'citizens' have and carry guns has become a frightening proposition. This thought process is not based on fact or personal experience, but upon feelings. The idea that other citizens might have a gun on their person creates a very real psychological discomfort and borderline panic in these people. To them, the perception that citizens should not have access to, nor carry, guns becomes, in their minds, a fact. They then take steps to ensure that this thinking, this self-imposed bias, becomes reality.

Here is an example. A good friend of mine is a television host and producer. A few years ago he signed a contract with a TV network (one of the big four broadcast channels) to air an outdoor/shooting sports television show during the network's "sports programming" time slot. My friend and his crew began taping, and they put together the season pilot to show to the network. This is when the wheels came off.

My friend's phone rang and on the other end was the programming V.P. of the network. He was upset and he was going to let my friend know why. "We can't air that on our network, you are teaching people how to hide guns on themselves." The comment stemmed from one segment of the show that discussed concealed carry. My friend tried to explain to the irate V.P. that the purpose of the spot was to discuss lawful concealed carry, a perfectly legitimate topic. "People cannot legally hide guns on themselves. That's against the law and we are not going to show people how to break the law."

In the end, the network V.P. was convinced, despite what my friend explained to him, that only police officers were allowed by law to "hide guns" and that there was no way in America that a citizen could legally hide a gun on their person. It was also forbidden by the network to shoot at cardboard targets that looked like the silhouette of a human; that would teach people to "murder". True story.

What we have in this case was a person who had decided, not based on research or fact, but on his own feelings, that no American could legally "hide a gun" on themselves. He would not be convinced by any argument that the opposite could be true. His feelings, based upon self-imposed bias, were all the reality he needed.

There Have Always Been Arms

To continue, whether we are discussing the club, the sword, the spear, bows (w/arrows), or a genuine firearm, for the entire recorded history of man there have been arms (weapons) available for his use. Consider the historical notion of the cave man, the Neanderthal; they are constantly depicted with a stick or club in their hands.

As man advanced, his weapon designs advanced as well. Native American Indians took the basic wooden club concept and enhanced it by using leather sinew to affix a stone to the end. They took the "war club" to new levels.

Without fail, as soon as a society discovered the use of bronze, iron, and steel they began to fashion more elaborate weapons out of metal. However, fabricating bronze or steel into a reliable and sturdy weapon required skill and, naturally, the monetary means to pay people to fabricate and craft these weapons.

It did not take long for the kings, emperors, lords, and other rulers to bring the skillful craftsmen and arms makers into their fold and control. A quality sword was both a thing of beauty and a symbol of authority for those who could attain it.

As handheld, man-portable weapons became more advanced and elaborate, a rift over who could afford them, and who should be in control of them, began.

Considering Rights

In our modern world, the words "rights" or "a right" are thrown about with reckless abandon. Everything that modern man has decided that he wants or desires has become some sort of "right". Many of these "rights" campaigns began as noble or worthy causes, but demand for rights have devolved into a most selfish acquisition.

We have had Women's Rights and Civil Rights campaigns. The Civil Rights Act of 1964 was noble and just at its core. Now we have splinter groups and factions claiming protection under the Civil Rights Act based not on their skin color or happenstance of birth, but upon the conscious choices they have made. The Civil Rights Act, rather than being an instrument to guard against institutionalized bias or oppression, is now wielded as a weapon to punish any person who might offend or disagree with some group claiming protection.

Every day there are news stories written where this right or that is put forth as a reason for the government, the state, to exercise control over free enterprise or the people themselves. Most recently, the manufactured concept of "healthcare rights" was used as an excuse for the state to meddle even further into the day to day health care of the people. We have witnessed disastrous results from furtherance of that so-called "right".

When the United States of America was founded, the populace recognized that the word "rights" was not one to be thrown around lightly. Several documents were written confirming the understanding that a true right was something "endowed by their Creator" and "inalienable". For instance, the Virginia Declaration of Rights, Article I states;

That all men are by nature equally free and independent, and have certain inherent rights, of which, when they enter into a state of society, they cannot, by any compact, deprive or divest their posterity; namely, the enjoyment of life and liberty, with the means of acquiring and possessing property, and pursuing and obtaining happiness and safety.

In the Virginia Declaration of Rights, unanimously adopted on June 12, 1776, the word "inherent" is used and that these rights *cannot, by any compact, deprive or divest their posterity.* For those who went to public school during the last twenty years or so, that means that a right cannot be taken away by the state or society and that it is a guarantee to your children and heirs.

As you will likely realize, Thomas Jefferson, a Virginian, closely mirrored the Virginia Declaration of Rights when he wrote the Declaration of Independence for the Continental Congress in July of 1776. The Bill of Rights, adopted in 1791, shares very similar phrasing to the Virginia Declaration. One might say that the Virginia document was the parent of both.

In the Declaration of Independence, paragraph 2 begins with;

We hold these truths to be self-evident, that all men are created equal, that they are endowed by their Creator with certain unalienable Rights, that among these are Life, Liberty, and the pursuit of Happiness. That, to secure these rights, Governments are instituted among Men, deriving their just Powers from the consent of the governed.

You will note that the "unalienable" rights, meaning cannot be taken away or denied, were natural rights given to all men when they were born as a gift by their Creator (capital "C") not by society or governments made of men. You should also note that these rights were few, not many. There are no health care rights, education rights, housing rights, cellphone rights, etc. in the founding documents.

At this point you may be wondering when I am going to get back to the subject of arms. Let us consider the right to bear arms in the founding documents of the United States. We will return to the Virginia Declaration of Rights, Article 13;

XIII That a well regulated militia, composed of the body of the people, trained to arms, is the proper, natural, and safe defense of a free state; that standing armies, in time of peace, should be avoided as dangerous to liberty; and that, in all cases, the military should be under strict subordination to, and be governed by, the civil power.

Again, you will see how the Virginia Declaration influenced the Bill of Rights in 1791;

Amendment II: A well regulated militia, being necessary to the security of a free state, the right of the people to keep and bear arms, shall not be infringed.

It was not just the Commonwealth of Virginia and the newly formed United States government that affirmed the right of the people to bear arms. Each individual, sovereign state has its own Constitution. Ohio thought that the right to bear arms was so important that they put it first, number one, in their Constitution in 1851.

The Constitution of the State of Ohio begins with a Bill of Rights;

ARTICLE I.

BILL OF RIGHTS

*Section 1. All men are, by nature, free and independent, and have certain inalienable rights, among which are those of enjoying and **defending life and liberty**, acquiring, possessing and protecting property, and seeking and obtaining happiness and safety.*

*Section 4. The people have the **right to bear arms for their defense and security**; but standing armies, in time of peace, are dangerous to liberty, and shall not be kept up; and the military shall be in strict subordination to the civil power.*

Wyoming simplified and clarified the question of the people bearing arms with one single sentence in its state Constitution; *Sec. 24. Right to bear arms.*

*The right of citizens to **bear arms in defense of themselves** and of the state shall not be denied.*

You will note there is no verbiage about "militias" that would allow anti-gun politicians to claim that only the "National Guard" should be allowed to have guns.

Lest you think that the "right to bear arms" was unique to the Revolutionary Generation of the 1770's, John Locke, a scholar of some note, wrote "A Letter Concerning Toleration" in 1689. Within this work we find that Locke addressed dealing with the evils of man;

But forasmuch as men thus entering into societies, grounded upon their mutual compacts of assistance for the defence of their temporal goods, may, nevertheless, be deprived of them by the rapine and fraud of their fellow citizens, or by the hostile violence of foreigners, the remedy of this evil consists in arms, riches, and the multitude of the citizens.

Over 100 years before the Bill of Rights for the U.S. Constitution was written, John Locke advised that the remedy for the citizens, the people, against the evil that men do, consisted in arms; ergo, the sword or the gun.

Considering that the founding documents of the United States of America, the sovereign States and the Colonies, all acknowledge and affirm the individual right of the citizen, the people, to keep and bear arms, we can see that it was an inalienable or inherent right. That is, one that cannot be taken away by the whims or will of any man. (*note: the use of the word "man" throughout denotes human, both male and female)

So, where does this leave us in the great enlightened age of endless rights, an era where everything the voter desires has become their right to have?

When you allow the state to create rights; health care rights, education rights, housing rights, cellphone rights, you accept and affirm that the state has the authority not only to oversee the distribution of those rights, but also the manner for which they are funded. The state is granted extra-Constitutional authority to decide who benefits from these new rights and who does not. Of course, as the distributor of rights, the state now has the authority to rescind previously existing arrangements and alter the rights distribution to their liking.

If we return to the original definition of rights, as inalienable and inherent, you will quickly realize that what has been advertised as a right is actually a state sanctioned privilege. Since the state is now in charge of deciding what is a right and what is not, who gets the right and who does not, you no longer have a government whose job is to secure and safeguard the inalienable rights of the people. You have returned to the time when the state dictates to the people what privileges they may and may not have.

When everything becomes a right, nothing is a right. That includes the right of the people to keep and bear arms. As the state has established the precedent of granting privileges under the guise of rights, the right to bear arms is now modified and no longer inalienable. Now the state can decide what arms the people may have and which ones are forbidden to them. The state can, at will, alter or amend previous arrangements. Arms that were common and lawful one day are illegal and forbidden the next day. We have seen this in the slippery slope of the National Firearms Act of 1934, the Gun Control Act of 1968, the Omnibus Crime Control Act of 1994. During each of these, the state altered and amended the previous agreement with the people and placed restrictions on their privilege to keep and bear arms.

Liberty and Freedom are not Interchangeable terms;
Liberty is the ability to make choices, freedom is a result of making the right choices.

"Being allowed to vote does not make a man free.
North Korea allows its people to vote. Saddam Hussein held elections in Iraq.
The right to vote is a byproduct of liberty.
Man cannot vote for liberty as liberty must come first.
Liberty must first be taken; it is secured and protected by men with arms.
To believe otherwise is to be childishly naive."
-PGM

Chapter 2   History of Arms Control

Those with very little understanding of history, or the desire to consider the world before they were born, believe that "gun control" is a modern, progressive movement by forward thinking, reasonable people. The current gun control movement is simply an extension of small arms control that has been around for centuries.

Consider the crossbow ban put into effect in Europe over 900 years ago. The Crossbow Ban was instituted by Pope Urban II in 1096 and upheld by Pope Innocent II in 1139. The secular leaders in Europe, for the most part, went along with the ban, at least when it came to fighting each other.

This is not surprising, as the crossbow, though arguably slow to load and reload, was aimed like a modern rifle and a peasant could be taught to use one in a relatively short period of time. Like the handguns and long guns that would arrive hundreds of years later, the crossbow put any able-bodied man, or woman, on equal footing with the King's, the Emperor's, or the Pope's soldiers. The idea that an ignorant peasant, by picking up a crossbow, could pierce the armor of a noble knight or lord must have terrified the ruling class at the time.

The more advanced handheld weaponry became, the greater the desire of the ruling class to restrict its ownership. Take, for instance the _Great Japanese Sword Hunt_ of 1588

The "Great Sword Hunt" of Toyotomi Hideyoshi is an instructive historical example of what can happen when the right to bear arms is taken away. Hideyoshi began his career as a lowly peasant spear-man in the armies of warlord Oda Nobunaga during Japan's Era of Warring States.

Working his way up to samurai status through his personal talent and strategic acumen, Hideyoshi eventually became one of Nobunaga's most important generals, and finally the dictator of medieval Japan. Considering his start as a peasant, you might think Hideyoshi would have been sympathetic with the condition of the lower classes, but then you would be failing to understand the mentality of a megalomaniac.

Hideyoshi's real concern was to make sure that no one else ever do what he had just done. So, he turned the previously fluid Japanese class system into a rigid caste system in which peasants would forever remain peasants with no possibility of ever being anything else. The one difficulty in enforcing this edict was an armed population, especially in those districts where rebellious leagues of peasants known as "ikki" had actually seized power from the ruling samurai.

Hideyoshi's solution was the "Great Sword Hunt," in which his soldiers went from town to town and house *to house confiscating swords, spears, guns and other weapons in order to disarm the population. The people were told that all of the weapons would be melted down and used to make a giant statue of the Buddha- which never happened. Instead, Hideyoshi launched two failed invasions of Korea with the ultimate goal of conquering Ming China.*

When he died, Japan collapsed into civil war once again- but the eventual winners of that war remained committed to Hideyoshi's policies. For the next three centuries, the common people of Japan had no choice but to obey their samurai masters or be cut down on the spot. They had been deprived of the means to effectively fight back.

The Chinese invention of gunpowder lead to the invention of the firearm some 500 years ago. Naturally, the first matchlocks, firelocks, and other man-portable guns were rather large, cumbersome and not at all cost effective.

Nonetheless, men will persevere and firearms became more reliable and easier for one man to carry and use effectively. Firearms quickly became an advantage of wealth and privilege. Take a tour of a natural history museum sometime and you will find intricately designed firearms that were as much artwork as weapon.

When the common man desired his own fowling pieces and deer guns, manufactures began to produce spartan and practical arms, minus the gold,

31

silver, and scroll work, for the masses. These spartan-looking guns also included handguns. This, my friends, is when the lords and ladies began to get nervous.

The common man, the peasant without land or title, could now possess the means to fight one on one with those sent to tax and enslave him. Firearms gave every man parity with every other man, regardless of title or government affiliation. Sam Colt is famous for inventing the handgun that became "the great equalizer".

Therein lay the problem. Those of title and nobility, those of the ruling class, were not at all enamored with the idea of the common man being on equal footing or having parity with the men they would send out to extract taxes and demand obedience. How can a lord feel confident that his commands will be obeyed without question when the peasants have the means at their disposal to resist said commands? The ruling class did not at all approve of the idea of a "great equalizer".

Throughout history there had been peasant and slave revolts and rebellions. However, very few were ever successful in the long term as the ruling class was always able to muster ample numbers to put down the revolt. The peasants and slaves had swords and spears. But those were up close and personal, hand to hand combat weapons.

The invention of the firearm and its subsequent falling into the hands of the common man meant that a rebellious serf or peasant could engage ruling class troops at a distance. Even men well beyond hand to hand or sword-fighting age could fire a gun.

This situation led to the first arms control restrictions and edicts against peasants and common people from owning weapons of war. Great Britain, being one of the largest empires during the age of firearms, soon began to issue edicts prohibiting firearms ownership by subjects it had colonized.

Officially sanctioned arms control by England was nothing new. The English crown forbade ownership of swords or other military arms by those it sought to control for hundreds of years.

The Disarming Act of 1745 followed the Disarming Act of 1716 and stated that Scotsmen were required to surrender their *"...Broad Swords, Targets, Poynards, Whingers or Durks, Side Pistol or Side Pistols Guns or any other Warlike Weapon."*

The edict was declared to be *"An Act for more effectual Disarming of the Highlands in that part of Great Britain called Scotland, and for better Securing the Peace and Quiet of that Part of the Kingdom..."*

*...the whole Highlanders without distinction are **disarmed forever and forbid** to use or bear arms under penaltys. (sp)* [Emphasis added]

Gun Control under the reign of the National Socialist German Workers' Party (Nazi for short) is often misunderstood as a complete and total confiscation of all firearms from all the people in Germany. American liberals like to call out pro-gun / pro-liberty factions in the United States for their blanket statements about Nazi gun confiscation. They say the pro-gun crowd is lying to generate fear of confiscation.

Actually, what took place was far more sinister. Firearms registration was indeed used by the National Socialists and their leader, Adolf Hitler, as a tool for confiscation of firearms, but not from everyone; just for the "politically unreliable." What that effectively meant was that Jews and other groups of German people who were not in direct line with the ruling Nazi party were deemed to be "unreliable" persons. Of course, the ruling party could not have people whom the state had labelled as "unreliable" in possession of firearms; that would endanger the safety of the community.

The National Socialist cleansing of German society and removal of guns from the hands of "unreliable" persons began in 1933 and continued for five years. Once labelled by the state as unreliable, thereby undesirable, the systematic removal of the disarmed people began in earnest. The undesirable, unreliable people were now outcasts in their own cities; their removal to special "work camps" became inevitable. Hitler's genocide record for killing "unreliable" persons stands between six and nine million, depending on the source.

In the Union of Soviet Socialist Republics (USSR), Joseph Stalin did not begin gun control, but followed the lead of Vladimir Lenin and the 1925 Criminal Code prohibiting the possession of arms by "unauthorized" persons. The USSR did not ban guns outright, they simply set in place a system whereby the ruling class state could decide who was authorized and who was not.

The combined death toll of Lenin and Stalin during their reign has been calculated in the tens of millions. That is a lot of dead "unauthorized persons".

Throughout the entire history of the arms or gun control movement, you will not find a state or ruling class that instituted a complete and outright ban of all arms within the country's borders. Instead what you will find across the board are laws and criminal codes that separate the humans in the nation into categories; those who cannot be trusted with unlimited possession of small arms and those who are exempt from those laws. The state and ruling class always exempt themselves from the laws applied to the "unreliable" or peasant class.

Lest readers would desire to give the United States a pass, consider the deceptively named; The Violent Crime Control and Law Enforcement Act of 1994. The bill was filled with prohibitions against the ownership of not only small arms, but accessories for those arms. Within the bill were detailed exemptions for employees of the Local, State, and Federal governments.

``(4) Paragraph (1) shall not apply to--
    ``(A) the manufacture for, transfer to, or possession by the
    United States or a department or agency of the United States or a
    State or a department, agency, or political subdivision of a State,
    or a transfer to or possession by a law enforcement officer
    employed by such an entity for purposes of law enforcement (whether
    on or off duty);

The 1994 Federal gun control bill was not new, it merely carried on the tradition of exempting certain persons of the state from the laws applied to the rest of the populace. On a national level, this behavior was codified in the National Firearms Act of 1934 and mirrored by every individual state gun restriction law.

When we consider the history of state sponsored arms control, we have to admit to the reality that arms control is a one-way street. The malum prohibitum statutes regarding arms only apply to certain subservient or peasant classes, the state is always exempt from the restrictions placed upon the subjects.

Consider the United Kingdom, a nation with some of the most restrictive firearms laws in the world. The people are completely without the rights or means to use guns in defense. British "Bobbies" are famous for their lack of arms. Nevertheless, after every terror attack in the U.K. we are treated to hundreds of photos of fully-armed British law enforcement personnel on every street corner. Even the famously anti-gun U.K. reserves the privilege of arms for members of the state.

Modern Movement

Socialist Venezuela passed strict gun control and prohibitions against the private ownership of firearms in June of 2012. Before that time, citizens could get a permit from the government and purchase firearms approved by the state. In 2012, the state changed its mind.

Just under five years later, the once prosperous and oil-wealthy nation of Venezuela was enveloped by food riots. During one riot, at least 12 starving people were killed fighting for food. Their economy destroyed by socialism, the disarmed and starving Venezuelan people fought back against the state crackdown on protesting by hurling feces at the security forces.

When we consider the history of arms control, we can see that it is a constant struggle to crush the spirit of man. For instance, when you consider the modern martial arts weapons that came from the Feudal Period of Japan, most all were tools or implements not seen as "weapons".

Throughout the world, people who have been disarmed by the state will come up with improvised weapons or will manufacture weapons in secret shops and trade them on the black market.

When a man flaunts the will of the state by making improvised black market weapons, he is classified by the state as a criminal. He is in possession of contraband items, those forbidden by his master to own. But, is this man truly a criminal at heart or is the possession of black market, secret arms an expression of man's spirit and desire to be free and independent?

To answer that question, we must consider the legal concepts of "Malum In Se" and "Malum Prohibitum". Malum in se is a moral wrong, or an act that is evil or wrong in and of itself. Members of a civilized society understand that murder, rape, theft, lies and deceit are wrong. We don't need to explain why murder and rape are wrong. Every member of a civilized society understands without explanation or coaching. Essentially, we are talking about numbers 4 to 10 of the Ten Commandments.

Malum prohibitum is a statute or edict that prohibits actions based upon the will or whim of the ruling class. For instance, the English prohibition against the Scottish owning swords, etc. was malum prohibitum, not malum in se. It was not a moral wrong for a Scotsman to own a sword, but the English king decided to forbid it, ergo malum prohibitum.

All gun control statutes and edicts are malum prohibitum. The ban on ownership of guns or certain kinds of guns is based on the will or whim of ruling class men. It is not evil or morally wrong for a man to possess arms. It is not a violation of God's law for a man to own a club, sword, or firearms. These restrictions only come from the desire of one man, or men, in an effort to restrict the behavior of, and control, another group of men.

"The rifle itself has no moral stature, since it has no will of its own. Naturally, it may be used by evil men for evil purposes, but there are more good men than evil, and while the latter cannot be persuaded to the path of righteousness by propaganda, they can certainly be corrected by good men with rifles."

- Col. Jeff Cooper (USMC Ret.) from his book The Art of the Rifle

Chapter 3   Psychological Control

As we have established, the modern gun control movement is simply an offspring of the concept of arms control and restrictions that has been around in one form or another for centuries. Let's take a moment to consider the history of arms control beyond the consideration of inanimate objects.

In truth, the desire of one class of people to restrict the ownership of arms by another class of people is as old as recorded history. When one group of people sets out to conquer and control another group, one of the first steps is to forbid the means of resistance by the conquered people. No swords for the conquered, or spears, lances, halberds, etc. Anything that could be considered a "weapon" is immediately forbidden.

More often than not, the penalty for the conquered peasant found in possession of a weapon was death; a very public execution so that the offending party could be made into an example. The message would be loud and clear to others; submit to your master, comply, do not resist.

The prohibition of arms, whether sword or gun, is just as much about psychology as it is physicality. Allow me to explain. When the state, the ruler, the master, forbids the peasants, the unreliable, to own the means of resistance, he is not only controlling the physical objects that they possess, he is also controlling their minds. He is forcing them to psychologically accept their position as a subservient class, a peasant class if you will. Disarmed people are part of the "unreliable" or "undesirable" class.

This makes a lot of sense when you consider that the physical means to resist are useless without the will or spirit to resist. It is far more beneficial for the ruler to control the mind of the peasant than the physical objects. The ruler must eliminate the very desire to possess and use arms to resist.

Once we have established that arms control or prohibitions are not based upon morality but upon the will and desires of one group to control another group, we can more deeply examine the psychology of arms control.

As we touched on earlier, the desire to own tools for self-protection or defense; clubs, swords, firearms, etc. is natural and common, going back as far as recorded history. Many in the world would have you believe that a man possessing a weapon is uncommon or an aberration. Even a brief review of natural history will destroy that assertion.

The world is full of threats to man's safety and has been since the beginning of time. Whether we are talking about the bear or the tiger or the rival tribe or bandits, man has always armed himself for the defense of his life and property. The attitude has been consistent, only the tools have changed.

All of the previous information leads us to the very real conclusion that arms control is about far more than the control of inanimate objects. If the state truly feared the existence of all arms and weapons, they could issue an outright ban on them. For everyone, not just for certain people.

When a man is disarmed via statute by the state, he has two choices; he can resist and continue to possess arms against the wishes of his master or he can submit to the wishes of his master and surrender the ownership of arms. Keep in mind we are not discussing the career criminal, the bandit, thief, or terrorist. The disarmed men of which we speak are citizens, members of some productive community, not social parasites and vermin.

As considered at the outset of this section, when the state finds a man in violation of its prohibition of arms, an example must be made. The conquered people must be shown that violation of the will of the ruling state will not be tolerated. A public display is made of the punishment of the man, or men, who have been caught violating the arms control statutes.

In days of old, a public execution was primary means of sending the message to the peasants. "If we catch you with a sword, you are going to be killed in front of your family and friends." Today, those who violate the King's arms control laws are not hanged or beheaded on the village green. No, today those accused of violating the state's arms prohibitions are tried and convicted by the news media in addition to the actual courts. The warning against violating the king's wishes is issued to the masses via their laptop computers or mobile phones. Subjects and peasants read stories of the fellow peasant convicted, fined, and jailed for breaking the king's arms rules.

As an added bonus, the state sympathetic media will often engage in character assassination of the accused. The subject convicted for violating arms control will be portrayed as a kook, as mentally unstable and a potential threat to the safety of the rest of the peasants. The media will cheer the conviction as an indication that the community will be "safer" now that the violator has been caught and punished.

Behind closed doors and in private conversations, the members of the modern ruling class understand that it is a literal impossibility to execute a forced disarmament of the subjects and unreliable people. The time and manpower required to search every home and building for arms could not be accomplished outside of the small village level, and even then, it would be a monumental task.

Instead, what the state seeks is psychological submission. Through the use of threats, random raids or "safety inspections", and the occasional public trial and persecution, the state is able to slowly but surely alter the thinking, or the psychology, of the conquered masses. The people that the state seeks to control will eventually succumb; not from a material standpoint, but from a psychological standpoint.

Rather than portray the prohibitions, raids/inspections, threats and executions as tyrannical or heavy-handed, the malum prohibitum edicts are put forth as a means to ensure the "safety" and "security" of the subjects. The English Arms Control Act of 1745 had as its stated goal *"...for better Securing the Peace and Quiet of that Part of the Kingdom... "*

The subjects are taught that they not only are not allowed to possess arms for defense, but that it is actually counter to their self-interest. Arms are dangerous to the subject or peasant and only the ruling class can be trusted to possess said arms.

Before long, we have peasants and slaves who not only fear to possess arms themselves, they will readily and happily turn in their fellow peasants for violation of the arms control edicts. Having accepted that arms are only for the state or ruling class, the psychologically converted peasants now view the state as their only protector. They have come full circle from their ancestors who understood that they needed a club to protect themselves from unforeseen threats.

The modern disarmed man blindly submits to the will of the state, as the state has now become his ultimate protector. All "safety" and "security" now flows from the king and the capital. The conversion of the man from a free and independent citizen to a dependent subject has been completed. The psychological transformation leading to submission, which was always the endgame of the state, has been realized. The people have been conquered and can now be easily controlled.

Disarming the Armed Citizen

Returning to the understanding by the modern ruling class that all-out, forced confiscation would be an impractical undertaking, and one that might lead to actual physical revolt, they have undertaken a more subtle tactic.

The problem for the modern ruling class elite is how to get peasants, already in possession of arms, to voluntarily accept more restrictions and get in line with the state's gun control program. The approach is threefold and has been ongoing for decades.

Ignorance

The first step is deliberate and purposeful ignorance. The people must be ignorant of history and historical facts. Natural history, the history of tyrannical behavior, the study of natural law and the rights of man are all watered down and eventually eliminated all together.

After a few generations, the people have no concept or understanding of the founding of their nations (particularly true in the United States). They will have no knowledge or understanding of the fate of the millions of people who submitted to arms control. They will accept arms control as a given that has always been accepted by the people of the nation.

Distraction

When combined with ignorance, distraction is used to keep the masses from being concerned about government overreach and instead focusing on meaningless and trivial subjects. During the downfall of the Roman Empire, the state used the device of "bread and circuses". Free bread and elaborate games and spectacles distracted the people from the fact that Rome had changed from a

Republic to an Empire. Today we have 24 hour a day sports channels and mobile phone apps to distract the masses. Sensationalism and tabloid journalism keeps the masses focused on the day-to-day activity of so-called celebrities and "reality" stars.

Naturally, the media is happily complicit in the distraction game. Thanks to cable television and satellite, we have 24 hour news channels to recycle the same stories endlessly.

The most modern form of 24/7 distraction comes from your handheld distraction device; your mobile phone. Using innumerable social media sites, you can now be distracted from sunrise to sunset.

Guilt

When ignorance and distraction are not enough to keep the masses from realizing government overreach, the tactic of guilt is employed. With a complicit media, sad stories of death and crime are forced into the faces of every citizen. News coverage of crime and injustice are run without end.

People who live thousands of miles away from the scenes of the crimes have the heinous details brought right to their living room or mobile phone. Self-appointed experts and government spokesmen offer their solutions; more state control, less independent liberty, for the safety of all.

Even before a crime or incident has been investigated and real information is available, news media experts take to the airwaves to offer speculation. The complete ignorance and bald faced media spin has been identified and called out numerous times. In 2016 Fox News engaged in total speculation laced with complete falsification. Fox brought on supposed expert, Jennifer Barringer, to offer speculation and deliver complete falsehoods in order to guilt the American people into accepting more gun control.

Ms. Barringer, supported by two Fox News women, went on national television and stated, without any idea whatsoever as to what firearm or firearms had been used to murder five police officers, that because there was a lot of hunting in Texas the gun laws were lax.

Barringer stated that the difference between a hunting rifle and an assault rifle is "the kind of scope you put on it". She further went on to say that such assault rifles were available for easy purchase at any "grocery store" and the attack could have been spontaneous as long as the gun was a "double shot weapon".

The entire segment, broadcast live on national television, had no basis in reality. The assertions of the "expert" were not only false, they were deliberately misleading lies. An informed and educated person could come away with only one conclusion; that Fox News segment was aired to scare the ignorant into demanding more government control of firearms.

Also, let us not forget the Operations Fast and Furious and Wide Receiver. With the blessing of the Obama Administration, the United States Department of Justice and the BATFE engaged in a program to deliberately funnel firearms into the hands of Mexican drug cartel members. The claim was that the DOJ and ATF would use weapons charges to bring down the cartels. During the ongoing operations, the Obama Administration touted the need for greater gun control to prevent violent drug dealers from getting ahold of the very guns they were funnelling to them.

The guilt scheme was exposed when Border Patrol Officer Brian Terry was killed with a gun that had been funneled by the ATF to drug gang members. Several books have been written exposing the government failure and corruption during this sponsored guilt campaign, including *Operation Wide Receiver: An Informant's Struggle to Expose the Corruption and Deceit That Led to Operation*

Fast and Furious. In the end, no drug cartels were "brought down" and very few charges were ever filed against low level gang members.

"... By disarming, you at once give offense, since you show your subjects that you distrust them, either as doubting their courage, or as doubting their fidelity, each of which imputations begets hatred against you."

— Niccolò Machiavelli, *The Prince*

Chapter 4   Criminals and Terrorists:

the Exemption and the Excuse

Thus far in our discussion, we have examined the king, the state, the ruling class, if you will, and the citizen, the subject or peasant, those who make up a productive community. A third element exists and that is the career criminal and the terrorist.

By career criminal, we mean a person who, by their history and behavior, is not a productive member of a culture or society, but instead is parasitic. The career criminal has made a life of leeching on the productive members of society through graft, deceit, theft, and robbery. Career criminals by nature have no regard for their victims; murder, extortion, assault, and rape are natural extensions of their antisocial behavior.

When we consider the terrorist, we are addressing those who do not wear the uniform of an opposing nation or operate under the structures and guidelines of conventional warfare. Terrorists operate autonomously and target both the state and the citizen alike. Unlike the career criminal, whose motivation is based upon greed and desire, the terrorist is more often motivated by ideology and the hatred of one class or culture.

Both the career criminal and the terrorist have in common the desire to harm and subjugate their

53

victims. Force of violence or the threat of violence are their primary means to achieve their ends. Possession of weapons quite naturally plays into the violence and threat of violence scenario.

When considering the behaviors of the criminal and terrorist, we can easily see that they are in violation of malum in se. Criminals and terrorists are morally wrong from the viewpoint of civil society, or at least the society that they have chosen as their victim.

The use of a prohibited weapon by the criminal/terrorist is merely an extension of the malum in se behavior. These vermin have already become comfortable with the idea of theft, robbery, rape, assault, and murder. Violating a state statute, or malum prohibitum, regarding arms is of little consequence to them.

Consider this from a rational viewpoint. You have a human creature whose mindset is such that they have justified the taking of an innocent human life as a part of their plan to get what they crave. Can we expect that a state prohibition against possessing some kind of inanimate object will dissuade them from their murderous desires?

In the case of the terrorist, we have one or more creatures, so filled with hatred for a target group that they will pre-plan a violent assault and murder of random people. Are we expected to believe that a state ban on arms will keep them from committing their assault?

All across Europe (France, Germany, England, Sweden etc.) we have witnessed ideological terrorists who, despite strict arms control laws, have improvised and used cars, trucks, kitchen knives, machetes, and hatchets to carry out their crimes. They have also received arms through networks of terrorist supporters. Witness the terror attacks in Paris, France.

If terrorists are gaining arms illegally through networks of supporters, how does a malum prohibitum statute restricting the citizens from owning a gun stop them? The answer is, it does not.

The spirit of evil of the terrorist, or career criminal, is such that they have slipped through the psychological control net put in place by the state via arms control. The criminal and terrorist are exempt from arms control as they do not fear public persecution and punishment. Weapons are a part of their tradecraft and they will purchase, steal, or improvise them in order to achieve their goals.

Despite a strict Arms Act in India, criminal gangs are supplied with weapons via underground arms factories in the jungle. Also, Australia, with its stringent arms control policies, has found that criminal gangs are simply making their own guns. The moral of the story is that a firearm is a simple machine that has been in existence for five centuries. Gun control laws aimed at disarming the people do nothing to stop the criminal and terrorist from getting and using firearms.

The great irony of the flaunting of malum prohibitum by the criminal/terrorist classes is the use of their actions and their existence by the state to justify more edicts and statutes. After horrific acts of barbarism and violence perpetrated by vicious career criminals or terrorists, the state, rather than admit that these monsters have exempted themselves from the king's rules, calls for more of the same failed policies. The answer to the failure of gun control is more gun control.

Gun Control in Prison

One of the greatest examples of the failure of arms control are prisons and the prison culture. Despite exercising the strictest control imaginable on the behavior of the residents, assault and murder, with improvised weapons, is commonplace in prison.

If arms control cannot even work in a maximum security prison, how can it be expected to work on a state level? The dirty secret is that it is not expected to work. The state understands that criminals and terrorists will always avail themselves to weapons;

this fact is irrefutable. That fact is also a moot point, as arms control is not aimed at the criminal or terrorist, it is aimed directly at the citizen, the ones who are not otherwise predisposed to break the law or violate malum in se.

Chapter 5   The Police Will Protect You

Prior to the modern era of human existence, say the last 200 years or so, there was essentially no distinction between the military and law enforcement. Taxes were collected by the king's or emperor's troops. There may have been magistrates or the shire-reeve, but the work of peacekeeping or peace-enforcing was accomplished by regular soldiers.

Consider the history of the original 13 Colonies of the United States. King George did not send policemen to enforce his edicts and collect taxes. Those chores were completed by the regulars, the red coats. When General Thomas Gage, the man who had replaced the Royal Governor Thomas Hutchinson in late 1774, ordered the arrest of John Hancock and Samuel Adams, he did not send patrolmen or deputies out of Boston, he sent the regular army.

Modern police departments, with armed men to enforce the peace, are relatively new in human history. It is the existence of these police agencies that has led many in the western world to use them as reasons for civilian disarmament. "You don't need a gun, we have the police." is a rallying cry for the pro-disarmament movement. Remember, the Gun Control movement is not anti-gun. They make allowances for the employees of the state to remain armed. It is only the unreliable citizen who cannot, and should not, be trusted with arms.

The "Police Will Protect You" mentality falls short on several levels and is easily destroyed when reason and facts are used to confront the fantasy and fallacy of that premise. From a practical standpoint, it is literally, not figuratively, impossible for any law enforcement agency to ensure that every single citizen, as well as their home and property, are protected from the previously mentioned career criminal and terrorist threat. The tax money required to hire enough police officers to act as the personal security guards for every home and business would bankrupt the nation.

The New York City Police Department, at this writing, has 34,000 plus uniformed officers. They are the largest single law enforcement agency in the United States. The census of NYC in 2016 was 8.5 million plus. That is one uniformed police officer for every 250 residents. So, using the "Police Will Protect You" logic, each NYPD patrolman would have to personally watch over and guard approximately 250 people.

What about the 911 system? Some would say that our modern emergency response system negates the need for individuals to possess arms for protection. Let us say that your community has 24/7 police patrols and a modern 911 dispatch system. Consider the following scenario:

It is 3 a.m. and your dog barks loudly. You wake up and realize that your back door has just been kicked in by an intruder, or multiple intruders. Grabbing the phone on the bedside table you dial 9-1-1. Fortunately, the operator picks up the phone after two rings. You state your name, your address and tell the operator someone has broken into your house. As they are required to do, the operator repeats back all you have said and then dispatches the nearest available car to your location. Total time elapsed, one minute to 90 seconds. The nearest patrol car to your home is 5 minutes away. Okay, you say, all is well. I will sit tight in my bedroom until the police arrive.

Keeping with the scenario, go to your backdoor, or front door, either one, open the stopwatch app on your mobile phone. Push start and walk through the door and continue to walk at a normal pace to your bedroom door. Hit the button and stop the timer. Unless you live in a mansion, it is a safe bet that you reached your bedroom door in well under the previously referenced 90 seconds. Any intruder could have been to your bedroom door before you could complete the call to 911, nevermind the 5 minute dispatch time.

"But, I have a lock on my bedroom door" you say, I got up and locked it before I called 911. If an intruder was able to kick in your back door, how long do you think a hollow-core interior door will keep them out? Are you alone in the house? Do you have children in bedrooms? What are your children going to do while you are hiding under the bed on the phone with 911?

That scenario was a home invasion where there was some time to react and call for help. What does the citizen do when the attack occurs away from home, out in public? When the moment arrives and you realize that one or more career criminals are going to attack you in public, your reaction time drops from 90 seconds down to a few seconds, two or three.

The previous were examples of the impracticality of the "police will protect you" mentality. The next impracticality comes from a legal standpoint.

In 1975, Carolyn Warren and her housemates were the victims of a home invasion and brutal sexual assaults and rapes in Washington, D.C. At the beginning of the incident, Warren called the Police Emergency number to report the home invasion. The police did respond to the residence, decided nothing was wrong, and left. Warren and two other women were sexually tortured for 14 hours.

Warren sued the District of Columbia claiming the police had failed in their duty to protect her and her housemates. In 1981, the United States Supreme Court sided with D.C. and ruled that the police had no "specific legal duty" to protect them as individuals, only in the general sense as members of the public.

This legal precedent was reinforced in 2005 after the estranged husband of Jessica Gonzales, whom she had a restraining order against, kidnapped and murdered her three children. Again, during the ensuing lawsuit, the court held that law enforcement officers have no constitutional requirement to protect an individual from harm.

Lest you believe that only the United States Supreme Court holds the "no duty" opinion, we have another example from New York City, home of 34,000 uniformed police officers.

On February 11, 2011, Maksim Gelman, murdered his stepfather with a kitchen knife during an argument. Gelman fled in his mother's car and in the process ran over a crossing guard. After his capture, Gelman stated that he knew he would be caught so he decided to take out "the rats" who had wronged him.

Maksim Gelman drove to the home of a girl he knew, Yelena, and stabbed her mother to death.

Yelena was not home so Gelman waited. During this time the NYPD was in search of Maksim for the murder of his stepfather.

When Yelena returned home, she found her mother dead and called 911. Before the police could arrive, Gelman returned, chased Yelena down and stabbed her to death. He fled the scene in a stolen car and ran down a pedestrian who later died of his injuries. Gelman also ran his stolen car into an occupied vehicle, got out and stabbed the driver, and stole that car.

Gelman abandoned the second stolen car around 1 a.m. on February 12, 2011. He flagged down a car occupied by two people, stabbed the driver multiple times and stole a third vehicle. Maksim Gelman abandoned the third stolen car and boarded a train at Lincoln Center, after he attacked and stabbed the ticket seller.

By the time he boarded the train, Gelman's picture was out in the news. Some passengers recognized him. Joseph Lozito was aboard the train, as were two NYPD officers inside of the operator's cab. According to several reports, Gelman tried to enter the operator's cab by banging on the door. The police inside told him to go away. Another passenger recognized Gelman and attempted to alert the officers, but he was ignored.

Maksim Gelman approached Joseph Lozito and reportedly said "You are going to die." and stabbed him immediately. Lozito leapt from his seat, fought with Gelman and was able to disarm him and pin him down after being stabbed and cut seven times. After the attack on Lozito began, NYPD officers left the operator's cab and arrested Gelman.

Joseph Lozito sued the City of New York and NYPD for negligence. Justice Margaret Chan, of the Manhattan Supreme Court ruled that Lozito could not sue for negligence because he did not directly contact the officers on the other side of the glass door and ask for their help. Again, the precedent cited is that police officers have no special duty to protect individuals, only the public in general.

What lessons can we learn from the Gelman case? The first lesson is obvious. Despite having 34,000 plus uniformed patrolmen, the NYPD could not stop or catch the killer during his 24 hour continuous rampage.

Secondly, with the exception of the two people run down by Gelman with a car, every victim had an opportunity, though brief, to produce a weapon and fight back. None of the victims were armed. New York City has an extremely restrictive licensing system for both handgun ownership and carrying. New York gun control is advertised as necessary for the safety of the people. In New York State, a citizen must get a permit to purchase a handgun, register the gun and themselves, and may only possess the specific handguns for which they are licensed to own. A knife attack is deadly force and the best defense against a sudden deadly force attack is a handgun carried at the ready. That is why the 34,000 NYPD patrolmen have handguns on their persons.

Lastly, the state has shown, on numerous occasions, that it cannot, and will not, expect state employees (police officers) to be the guardians or protectors of individual citizens. This is true even when they are present during the commission of the crime such as we witnessed in the Gelman case.

Chapter 6   Guns for Rebels and Freedom

Fighters, Not for Citizens

In Warsaw, Poland, near the POLIN Museum, there
stands an enormous monument dedicated to the
heroes of the Warsaw Ghetto Uprising. Every year
visitors come and pay their respects, lay wreaths
and leave flowers. Visiting heads of state and
diplomats are known to visit the monument for the
obligatory photo op. Numerous speeches have been
delivered extolling the virtue of the jewish men and
women who rose up against their Nazi oppressors
and fought back during the Warsaw Ghetto
Uprising of 1943.

Presidents and Prime Ministers will stand before the
monument and pontificate about the bravery of
those who, despite overwhelming odds, stood up
against the National Socialist invaders. These same
politicians will use words like "sacrifice" and
"inspiration", "courage" and "bravery" when
describing the people who fought to their ultimate
deaths in Warsaw. Those world leaders who do
acknowledge the Holocaust, will use words such as,
"never forget" and "vigilance". The masses are
reminded that mankind must never allow such
circumstances to occur again. Of course, these same
leaders rarely acknowledge the mass starvation and
gulag deportation of Stalin's USSR. Neither do they
reference the millions of citizens who died in

communist China or in the killing fields of Cambodia where two million citizens were slaughtered.

Who were the people who fought back in Warsaw? The men and women who took up arms against German government troops, employees of the state, in Warsaw were not soldiers or members of a sanctioned military organization. The Jews of the Warsaw Ghetto were *forbidden* to possess arms, as they were unreliable people. By picking up guns and attacking the uniformed members of a sanctioned state military, these people were breaking the law. Yet, despite that fact, decades later, world leaders stand in front of a monument to those who violated gun control laws and praise their efforts.

Is it ironic or hypocritical, or both, that most all of the leaders who will publicly praise the bravery of the Jews in the Warsaw Ghetto come from countries that have severe restrictions regarding civilian gun ownership, especially "military style" weapons? From one side of their mouths they extol the virtues of fighting back against the forces of National Socialism (Nazi for short) and from the other side they spout the public safety argument for strict gun control.

For example, in July of 2016, Canadian Prime Minister Justin Trudeau paid a visit to Auschwitz, a death camp where many of those who survived the Nazi ghettos were sent to be exterminated. Trudeau wrote the following words in the guest register. *"Tolerance is never sufficient; humanity must learn to love our differences. Today we bear witness to humanity's capacity for deliberate cruelty and evil. May we ever remember this painful truth about ourselves, and may it strengthen our commitment to never again to allow such darkness to prevail. We shall never forget."*

In addition to his words being pithy and meaningless, Trudeau is a hypocrite. The Canadian government is proud of its strict gun control laws. You see, the citizens of Canada are much like the "unreliable" people who fell under the control of the government of the National Socialist German Worker's Party.

In Canada, most all citizens are banned from owning semi-automatic rifles and handguns. They cannot possess military style "assault weapons" without strict government scrutiny and inspection. Essentially, Canadian citizens can have some guns to play games, but not to fight. Apparently, Trudeau believes that an over abundance of tolerance and a love for the differences of humanity will stop the next holocaust.

Canadian gun control and Trudeau's "peace, love, tolerance" speeches did not stop the ISIS inspired jihad attacks in Quebec and Ontario. Perhaps the muslim missionaries were simply unaware that they were violating gun control restrictions.

The United States government has a long history of sending arms to "freedom fighters" and "rebels". From China, to Central America, to Afghanistan, to other places in Africa and the Middle East, the U.S. government has a long track record of sending military hardware; battle rifles, machine-guns, grenades, rocket launchers, etc., not to sanctioned military organizations, but to unsanctioned groups made up of citizens of the region. Once this hardware is on the ground and distributed, the U.S. supplier loses complete control over who gets or uses it, but the stated hope is that the rebels will fight for the freedom of the people.

Contrast the willing desire of the United States and other countries to hand off weapons of war to rebels and freedom fighters, to the current United States gun control laws and the policies put in place and monitored by the BATFE.

Since 1934, no United States citizen can own a firearm capable of fully-automatic fire without first seeking permission from the state. That edict was expanded in 1986 to prohibit any firearm built after that date, ergo "no new machine-guns".

The BATFE discovered language that does not exist in the United States Constitution nor Bill of Rights when they decided to begin using the phrase "legitimate sporting purpose". No firearm can be imported into the United States and sold to the peasants unless our masters have determined that you can play a game with it. If the gun is only for fighting, it is forbidden.

So, what we have here is a pattern of the United States Federal Government using the tax money taken from its citizens to fund programs to send military small arms to foreign national citizens, rebels and freedom fighters, while at the same time denying ownership of any such items by United States citizens. The American taxpayer is responsible enough to fund these programs, but not responsible enough to benefit from them.

Consider the horrible mess we allowed Comrade Barry Hussein Soetoro to put us in. Comrade Barry green lit CIA programs to arm Islamic freedom fighters in northern Africa and the Middle East. Almost immediately, those military arms, of which the American people are forbidden to own, were turned on our allies and our own troops in the region.

The Eunuch wants His Testicles Back

During the late-unpleasantness that is the unchecked jihad committed by muslim missionaries against the people of Europe, many news reports have been written relating the desire of the disarmed people to get their "gun rights" back. Numerous jihad attacks against the people of Great Britain have shown the residents that their government has done little to nothing to prevent the murders from happening and they, like American police, can only respond after scores have been killed. British citizens want a repeal of the handgun ban and a re-opening of "shooting clubs".

In Germany, where firearms ownership is strictly regulated, the people are scrambling to find ways to arm themselves. Again, innumerable jihad attacks against the people have shown that the government is not capable of protecting the people as individual citizens. Despite strict gun control, muslim missionaries are killing scores of German citizens. Ironically, for a German citizen to own a firearm capable of self-defense, they must beg the state for permission to do so.

The failure of stringent gun control policies in France has been put on display. The people must follow strict guidelines to acquire and own a gun, but terrorists showed that they have little trouble getting ahold of firearms with which to commit mass murder.

Conversely, the Czech Republic has taken a public stance against jihadist and muslim missionaries. Czech President, Milos Zeman, told the people of that country that it is their responsibility to be armed to fight terrorists. That move was scorned by the rational and reasonable leaders of the European Union.

"It is seldom that liberty of any kind is lost all at once.

Slavery has so frightful an aspect to men accustomed to freedom that it must steal in upon them by degrees and must disguise itself in a thousand shapes in order to be received."

-David Hume, <u>Of the Liberty of the Press</u>

Chapter 7   Reversing Gun Control

Having come to this point in the text, the reader must make a conscious mental decision. Many readers will conclude that, though there is demonstrable historical evidence that a disarmed populace cannot be protected from the evil of the criminal and terrorist, nor the tyrannical overreach of the state itself, a country where the people are disarmed is safer.

In a way, the final portion of the previous statement is true. Okay, to be fair, the statement is partially true. In a country where the people are disarmed (the state will never disarm) violent criminals, terrorists, street gangs and thugs are much safer. The aforementioned monsters will fear no reprisal from their victims.

It is also true that the Gestapo, the Stasi (ask your elders), the Soviet KGB, and other Secret Police representatives of the state were/are much safer knowing that when they kicked/kick down a door at 3 a.m. the people on the other side would be/will be safely disarmed.

Life must have been safer for the feudal lords, barons, and kings after the peasants were all disarmed by force or threat of death. Tax collectors could fleece the masses with little fear of resistance.

So, in a way, yes, if safety for the representatives of the state, as well as those who live and operate outside of the realm of law is your goal, a disarmed populace is a good start. Crushing indebtedness and taxation is another way to pacify and control the masses, but that is a topic for another day.

As we have pointed out previously, when faced with an unending threat of murder and mayhem by those operating outside of the law, the people of the United Kingdom, France, Germany, and other socialist countries have begun to clamour for "gun rights". But, how do you reattach the testicles to the eunuch?

How do you reverse a decades old campaign to vilify firearms, at least in the hands of the people? Remember, guns in the hands of the state are acceptable and necessary. Since before most of the inhabitants of modern Europe were born, the aforementioned socialist states have engaged in well-organized propaganda programs to not only reinforce their disarmament policies, but to make people fear the possession of arms.

Throughout much of the world, firearms are quaint tools for hunting and participating in state approved sporting events. The arms that the peasants are allowed to possess are strictly scrutinized, restricted, and effectively neutered so as to have only minimum potential value as a fighting tool.

The most effective tools for self-reliance; handguns and self-loading rifles, are forbidden to the socialist peasant.

(Note: If the term "peasant" offends, then you must believe it has a ring of uncomfortable truth. Rather than vent anger at the author of a book, perhaps you might vent some useful anger against the political system that has relegated you to tax peasant status, but I digress.)

Time and again we are treated to interviews of people who live in countries where firearms ownership is strictly controlled and only licensed sport and hunting is allowed. The idea of using a firearm as a fighting tool is as foreign or ludicrous to them as that of flapping your arms and taking flight.

Imagine if you will, a country where the state has engaged in a 50 year campaign to convince the people that large bodies of open water are dangerous, a hazard to the community at large. Afterall, children have drowned in water and one child's death is one too many. Entering a lake or the ocean is forbidden by law and a punishable offense. Citizens who had dared to test the waters were tried and convicted in a public fashion. The media ran stories warning the citizens to beware of these "water-nuts". State hotlines were set up so good citizens could anonymously report on their neighbors who might be "water-lovers".

Then, one day the state says, "Everyone is going to learn how to swim, jump in the pool". There would be abject panic amongst the water-fearing populace. People would beg and plead with the state to protect them from the water. Coalitions would be formed to lobby the state for even greater water control, for the safety of all.

How can you reverse generations of "guns are bad" thinking? How do the people, who might be asking for the physical means of self-protection, go from "firearms are evil and dangerous" to a gun is a tool that you must learn to master?

More importantly, how do the inhabitants of a state where gun control is the law of the land convince the ruling class, the political elite, to change the laws and let them have their "gun rights back"?

The ruling class and political elite are not affected personally by firearms restrictions. Politicians and the wealthiest and most influential members of society are protected from lawlessness by armed agents of the state or by duly licensed bodyguards. The aforementioned elite fear no street crimes or home invasions.

Also, and this is a big also, when a populace has been disarmed and they become afraid, whether from criminals or terrorists, they have no recourse but to plead with the state for protection. The monopoly of arms gives the ruling class tremendous power. Why, once it has been gained, would a politician ever relinquish that amount of power over their subjects?

Remember, after every incident of terror, no matter where it happens to take place, the first reaction of the state is to send men in uniform with guns out to stand on every street corner. Heavily armed police officers mill about at every major intersection and thoroughfare. Why? To stop future terrorist attacks? No. These men (and women) are there to make the peasants feel safe. The sight of hundreds of uniformed agents of the state standing around is supposed to indicate to the populace that all is well and that the state has matters in hand.

How has this security theater worked for the people of Europe during the last decade? We see a schizophrenic "Rinse, Lather, Repeat" pattern. A terror attack occurs, hundreds of cops mill about on the streets for a few days, politicians swear to "bring those responsible to justice", people get comfortable again, and you have another terror attack.

One item that we can now add to that list is "citizens seek return of gun rights". If the demand for gun rights lasts for more than a week or so, the state will amp up the number of news stories that show how hard they are working to break up the terror network or arrest those responsible for the atrocities. Politicians may even feign support and promise to look into returning some gun rights, in a rational and reasonable fashion of course. But, alas, in the end, even these favorable politicians cannot or will not deliver on their promises and the people are right back to square one; unarmed victims.

Petitions and referendums you say, that is the answer. You will gain ample signatures and force the ruling class to hear your voice. You may even organize to the point where you force a voter referendum to put a measure on the ballot to regain your gun rights, if you even have that option.

 If the Gun Rights movement appears to gain any kind of traction, without fail, the ruling class will encourage the mainstream media to ramp up their gun fear editorials. Stories will air about the alarming number of accidental deaths with firearms in places where people are allowed to own guns. You will be treated to heretofore unheard of research reports that you are 537 percent more likely to kill yourself with a gun than you are to use it to defend yourself. Gun ownership will be linked to a rise in suicide, murder, rape, robbery, unwanted pregnancy, syphilis and gonorrhea.

Psychologists and psychiatrists will issue forth grim warnings that the desire to own a firearm is unhealthy and a strong indicator of mental incompetence. Anyone, other than agents of the state, with a strong desire to own a gun should be treated for mental health issues and will definitely need to be monitored closely so they do not harm others or themselves.

Finally, as we have witnessed far too often in the United States of America, if the Gun Rights movement does indeed succeed with a voter referendum to force the state to ease gun control laws, the ruling class will simply go judge shopping and find a reliable court to issue an immediate sanction against the referendum and then it will eventually be declared unconstitutional.

I fully understand that I am painting a grim picture and I do not do so to be confrontational or to belittle the effort. The fact is that no state or ruling class has ever reversed its position on gun control and civilian disarmament of its own volition. Why would they ever voluntarily surrender that level of power and control over the people?

The American Revolution, although this fact is glossed over in popular retellings of history, began because of the state's attempt to institute gun control. Paul Revere and William Dawes rode out to the Massachusetts countryside to warn the people that the Regulars (not British, the colonists considered themselves to be Sovereign British Citizens) were coming.

What was the mission of the Regulars (Redcoats) on April 19, 1775? Their mission was to find and arrest John Hancock and Samuel Adams and to seize and/or destroy "arms, powder, and military stores" in the hands of the people of Concord. The Regulars burned and destroyed a fair amount of property that they deemed could be used by rebels on their march from Lexington to Concord.

This was not the first attempt by the Royal Governor to seize arms from the people, it was actually the third, the first two being largely unsuccessful. You see, despite the "Boston Massacre" of 1770, the Stamp Act, Tea Act, and the "Intolerable Acts", the American Revolution did not become a shooting war until the state decided that it was time to take away the guns and ammunition from the people.

When the people fired back in open revolt, the British Crown did not see the error of their ways and recant, they doubled down with thousands of additional troops and hundreds of ships to enforce their will. It took eight full years to secure and re-establish the rights of the people, including the right to keep and bear arms.

Additionally, even after the blatant attack against the people of Massachusetts by the Regulars, eight were killed and ten wounded on Lexington Green, not to mention the torching of homes and businesses, many colonists still favored the promised safety and security of the British Crown.

Loyalists and Tories turned on their fellow citizens, they informed on the "gun nuts" and "freedom lovers" of that time. They turned over the names of their neighbors to the state. In areas controlled by Regular troops, these pro-freedom citizens were arrested, many were hanged as an example, and thousands imprisoned only to die during the horrors of incarceration.

Gun Rights and individual liberty in the United States of America was bought and paid for, not with petitions and referendums, they had been petitioning the King and parliament for years, but with the blood of thousands of men and women. Historians believe over 24,000 men died in battle and thousands more died while being held prisoners of war.

The greatest hindrance to the return of gun rights to a populace that surrendered them long ago is not the actual laws forbidding ownership. No, the greatest stumbling block is the mindset of the people themselves. When the unarmed populace has been regularly abused by hyper-violent, foreign-born monsters, as in the case of Europe, they look at guns as some kind of quick fix. If only they had a gun, it would be different. What they fail to see is that where people are genuinely free, a firearm is an instrument of liberty. A gun is not a magic talisman to ward off evil.

By and large, the people living in socialist countries were not disarmed by force. They were disarmed mentally, they voluntarily surrendered their gun rights for the empty promise of safety from the state. Before you open up the armories and start passing out rifles, the mindset of the people must be changed. They must see arms as instruments to preserve individual liberty and that liberty includes the prerequisite of responsibility, a responsibility to be self-sufficient.

A man cannot look to the state as the source of all fairness, equality, and security while at the same time pledging to arm himself for his own defense. It does not work that way. The state will never willingly share power with the peasants after they have achieved such a great level of power.

In case my message has not been clear, what I am saying is that until the people refuse the opiate of "fairness and safety" that the state is offering, until they are ready to accept responsibility for their own well-being, their successes and failures, there is no hope at all that they will enjoy "gun rights".

As long as you reside in a nanny state, a socialist paradise, where the people exist to provide tax revenue to a leviathan state, there is little hope that you will ever be "allowed" by the state to arm yourself for the purpose of self-defense. Armed citizens and socialist states cannot coexist.

Epilogue Dancing in the Blood of the Innocent

As the final draft of this text was being prepared, the Las Vegas massacre and the Sutherland Springs, Texas Church attack took place. As if on cue, socialist politicians and self-deluded Hollywood types raced each other to the microphones and Twitter accounts to dance in the blood of the innocent in order to push their sick agenda.

The definition of terrorism is; the use of violence, particularly against civilians, in order to advance a political agenda. With no historical or factual evidence to support their claims, the aforementioned vermin pushed for immediate legislation to further disarm those who are actually the victims of attack. Remember, murder is illegal in the United States. More state control is not the answer to the problem of human evil. We are supposed to believe that evil behavior can be curtailed if the people would only surrender even more liberty to the will of the state.

In the case of the Sutherland Springs murders, the suspect was prohibited by law from owning a firearm. The government failed to meet its obligation to prevent the sale when the obligatory background check was conducted. The Malum Prohibitum law failed. We also know that the murderous rampage was stopped by the intervention of, not one but two, armed citizens, not the police.

Despite the glaring failure of gun laws, as well as an inability of police to prevent attacks, coupled with the positive actions of armed citizens, the usual suspects are calling for more laws and fewer armed citizens.

Law enforcement officials keep saying that they can find no motive for the Las Vegas attack. However, when I was a police officer many moons ago, one of the investigative tools we learned was that when there seemed to be no motive for a crime, take a step back and see just who it was that would or could benefit from the crime.

The mainstream media of the United States has long since pledged their allegiance to socialist democrats and all of their progressive causes. No hard questions will be asked and no proof that new gun laws will actually work will be sought. Throngs of soy-fed manginas and spineless millennials, who have never had to accept responsibility for any action they take, echo the sentiments of the state who they view as the arbiter of all that is fair in the world.

Deep inside their black souls, the ruling class elite know that additional Malum Prohibitum laws cannot stop evil men from doing evil things. Conversely, the soy-fed, emotionally driven masses look for the quick answer; ban all guns, as if evil men will comply with their wishes and not arm themselves to further their evil deeds.

The disturbing fact is that the more successful progressive socialists are at using terrorism to push their agenda, the more those attacks will occur. These attacks on innocent civilians are designed to frighten or terrorize the people into surrendering liberty for the promise of state provided safety. When politicians push for more government control while using vicious terror as the reason, they are literally, not figuratively, guaranteeing that more of the same will take place.

My friends, the solution to evil is not capitulation, weakness, and surrender; the solution to evil is strength and the resolve to fight evil. I would ask you to pray that the good people of this world find the strength to fight evil.

Sources and Reference Material

European Crossbow Ban
http://militaryhistorynow.com/2012/05/23/the-crossbow-a-medieval-wmd/

Great Sword Hunt in Japan
http://politicsreport.com/article/great-sword-hunt

Scottish Disarmed
http://www.tartansauthority.com/resources/archives/the-archives/scobie/tartan-and-the-dress-act-of-1746/

English Gun Control
http://www.nationalarchives.gov.uk/education/resources/jacobite-1745/9128-2/

National Socialist Gun Control
http://www.nationalreview.com/article/365103/how-nazis-used-gun-control-stephen-p-halbrook

Soviet Socialist Firearms Restrictions
https://www.researchgate.net/publication/228264208_Lethal_Laws

Venezuela Gun Control
http://www.bbc.com/news/world-latin-america-18288430

Food Riots kill 12 in Venezuela
https://www.nytimes.com/2017/04/21/world/americas/venezuela-riots.html

Venezuelan People throw Feces
https://www.hrw.org/blog-feed/venezuelas-crisis

Operation Fast and Furious Exposed
http://www.foxnews.com/politics/2017/06/07/fast-and-furious-report-slams-holder-doj-for-deception-in-gun-running-scandal.html

Illegal Arms Factories, India Jungle
http://www.business-standard.com/article/specials/gun-violence-and-illegal-arms-in-india-115101900035_1.html

Australian Homemade Machineguns
http://www.abc.net.au/news/2016-11-23/queensland-police-find-sophisticated-gun-manufacting-workshop/8051244

Police have no legal duty to protect individuals
http://law.justia.com/cases/district-of-columbia/court-of-appeals/1981/79-6-3.html

http://www.nytimes.com/2005/06/28/politics/justices-rule-police-do-not-have-a-constitutional-duty-to-protect.htm

http://nypost.com/2013/01/27/city-says-cops-had-no-duty-to-protect-subway-hero-who-subdued-killer/

http://www.nydailynews.com/news/crime/subway-stabbing-victim-sue-city-cops-didn-stop-attack-article-1.1409451

Warsaw Ghetto Uprising

https://www.ushmm.org/wlc/en/article.php?Module
Id=10005188

24,000 killed during the American Revolution

https://www.civilwar.org/learn/articles/american-re
volution-faqs

Of Liberty of the Press, David Hume

http://www.constitution.org/dh/libpress.htm

About the Author

Paul G. Markel has worn many hats during his lifetime. He has been a U.S. Marine, Police Officer, Professional Bodyguard, and Small Arms and Tactics Instructor. Mr. Markel has been writing professionally for law enforcement and firearms periodicals since 1993 with hundreds upon hundreds of articles and several books in print.

Mr. Markel is an Amazon Best-Selling author, previous contributor to The Blaze, and frequent guest on radio and television programs.

Paul is also the host and producer of Student of the Gun TV and Radio. Mr. Markel is the founder of Student of the Gun University, an entity dedicated to education and enlightenment.

For more information, please visit
www.studentofthegun.com

Additional Books by Paul G. Markel

<u>Patriot Fire Team Manual</u>

<u>Faith and the Patriot: A Belief worth Fighting For</u>

<u>The Intolerant Christian</u>

<u>Team Honey Badger; Raising Fearless Kids in a Cowardly World</u>

<u>Dad Rules, Wit and Wisdom from a Dad To Whom it May Concern</u>

<u>Cigar Etiquette for Barbarians</u>

<u>Event Security: Getting Ready for the Big Day</u>

All books are available on Amazon.com as paperback and Kindle editions

Also, follow us at:

www.StudentoftheGun.com

www.PatriotFireTeam.com